SUDDEN POSITION GUIDE TO

Collection Management

ALCTS SUDDEN POSITION SERIES

Guide to Cataloging and Metadata, #1
Jeremy Myntti, Editor, 184 pp. 2019.
ALCTS, ISBN: 978-0-8389-4857-6

ALCTS SUDDEN POSITION SERIES #2

SUDDEN POSITION GUIDE TO Collection Management

Becca Brody

SUSAN E. THOMAS ■ SERIES EDITOR

Association for Library Collections & Technical Services
a division of the American Library Association
CHICAGO 2020

The paper used in this publication meets the minimum requirements of American National Standard for Information Sciences—Permanence of Paper for Printed Library Materials, ANSI Z39.48-1992.

ISBNs
978-0-8389-4664-0 (print)
978-0-8389-4665-7 (pdf)

Library of Congress Cataloging-in-Publication Data
Names: Brody, Becca, author.
Title: Sudden position guide to collection management / Becca Brody.
Description: Chicago : Association for Library Collections & Technical Services, a division of the American Library Association, 2020. | Series: ALCTS sudden position series ; #2 | Includes bibliographical references and index. | Summary: "While the terms "collection management" and "collection development" are used interchangeably by many people in the library profession, collection management can be seen as a somewhat broader term, encompassing maintenance of the physical collection, usage assessment, and policy development, as well as preservation and storage activities, planning for space reclamation, and the execution of other collections-focused projects within the library. While collection development and acquisitions can be seen as part of the collection management process, the Sudden Position Guide to Collection Management focuses on aspects of collection management that do not deal directly with the process of selecting and acquiring materials for the collection. Instead, the focus will be on how to manage physical and digital items that are already a part of the library's holdings"— Provided by publisher.
Identifiers: LCCN 2019055532 (print) | LCCN 2019055533 (ebook) | ISBN 9780838946640 (trade paperback) | ISBN 9780838946657 (pdf)
Subjects: LCSH: Collection management (Libraries)
Classification: LCC Z687 .B76 2020 (print) | LCC Z687 (ebook) | DDC 025.2/1—dc23
LC record available at https://lccn.loc.gov/2019055532
LC ebook record available at https://lccn.loc.gov/2019055533

Printed in the United States of America

24 23 22 21 20 5 4 3 2 1

Contents

Foreword

The *Sudden Position* series began with an idea from Mary Miller, Director of Collection Management and Preservation at the University of Minnesota, who was serving as the chair of the ALCTS Publications Committee. She suggested creating a monographic series similar to the ALCTS Collection Management Section (CMS)'s *Sudden Selector's Guide* series, but instead of focusing on resources, it would focus on the task of positions. As our profession evolves, many of us have experienced being asked to take on additional responsibilities. I found myself in this position over twelve years ago when one year into a new position managing collection development, I was asked to take on the responsibility for acquisitions. This was a new area for me, and I looked to ALCTS to help me get up to speed. I enrolled in the Fundamentals of Acquisitions web course, which I found extremely valuable in helping me to understand and take on this new responsibility. The *Sudden Position* series, like the Fundamentals web courses, is intended to provide the reader with essential knowledge, tools of the trade, and best practices in a concise, easy to read and reference narrative format. The guides are specifically meant to help anyone who is taking on a new position or added technical services responsibility.

Susan E. Thomas
ALCTS Monographs Editor
March 2019

Acknowledgments

I'd like to thank several people without whom this book would not have made it beyond an outline: my current and former library colleagues at Westfield State University who listened to my ideas and offered suggestions—particularly Ed Hill, Corinne Ebbs, and Oliver Zeff; library director Tom Raffensperger who encouraged me to write for publication in the first place; Susan Thomas, ALCTS Monographs Editor, for shepherding me through the submission process; and my partner, Ben Brody, who endured perhaps one too many dinners where I discussed the finer points of ADA-compliant aisle clearance.

INTRODUCTION

So You're Suddenly a Collection Manager

Librarians become collection managers for a variety of reasons. Some take over the position after working in another capacity within the library. Some are new hires who have never worked as a collection manager before. Others are tasked with a particular collection project and need a crash course in how to approach weeding, database evaluation, or space reclamation. While there are excellent, in-depth treatments of the theory and practice of collection management,[1] this monograph focuses on the practical, nuts-and-bolts issues, and essential knowledge every collection manager needs to perform well in an evolving environment.

WHAT IS COLLECTION MANAGEMENT?

While the terms "collection management" and "collection development" are used interchangeably by many people in the library profession,[2] collection management can be seen as a somewhat broader term,[3] encompassing not only collection development but also housing and maintenance of the physical collection, usage assessment, policy development, preservation and storage activities, planning for space reclamation, and the execution of other collections-focused projects within the library such as shifting, relocation, storage, and weeding. The broadest definition of collection management encompasses virtually anything a library worker might do in relation to library materials, from initial selection to eventual deaccession and everything in between. The collection manager frequently makes strategic recommendations regarding format, storage, selection, and deselection of collection materials.

INSIDE THIS GUIDE

This guide focuses on aspects of collection management that do not deal directly with the process of selecting and acquiring materials for the collection.[4] These activities are worthy of a separate monograph. Instead, this volume focuses on how to manage physical and digital items that are already a part of the library's holdings. In addition, the specifics of print serials management—including checking in, subscription review, claiming, and maintaining accurate holdings—are beyond the scope of this book.

Chapter 1 focuses on the critical job responsibilities and functional areas of collection management. Competence in these areas requires knowledge of relevant collections standards, outlined in chapter 2. Chapter 3 details things you might encounter related to documentation and the management of print and electronic collections. The tools and skills needed to accomplish collection management tasks are covered in chapter 4. The resource list in chapter 5 provides suggestions for further reading, online courses, conferences, and other methods of professional development. Free and low-cost opportunities for improving collection management skills abound. Both the notes and resources sections include important professional organizations in the fields of collection management, preservation, and related activities. The included listings are intended to provide an entry point to the professional literature related to this area of librarianship.

CURRENT COLLECTION MANAGEMENT LANDSCAPE

Libraries have been evolving rapidly as the world adjusts to the explosion of online information sources, both on the open web and in proprietary, subscription-based resources. Collection managers must stay abreast of developments in online resources and data management while also responding to the increasing demand for electronic resources. The effect that the shift from print to digital has on library collections, spaces, budgets, and both short- and long-term collection management strategy is a primary focus of modern collection management. Increasingly vendors that have traditionally provided materials for a fee are making some materials open access. Library users of all stripes are also demanding more access to streaming video and eBooks. Once these materials are part of the collection, they must be managed and maintained—and ideally assessed—for continued relevance and cost-effectiveness, like any other resource.

Librarians face a landscape in which cost increases routinely outpace inflation while budgets increase nominally, if at all. Library users, however, still want a high level of service and expect the library to be able to provide materials quickly in their preferred formats. For some users, this means electronic resources that are easy to download to e-readers and mobile devices; for others it means print materials and physical media. In addition, users want library collections to be accessible, relevant, and well-organized.

Space Reclamation and Repurposing

Many types of libraries are facing an increased demand for repurposing physical space which puts pressure on areas traditionally dedicated to housing library collections. Libraries are now expected to provide space for support services such as writing centers, computer and media labs, group study areas, meeting rooms, maker spaces, and cafes. Library space reclamation projects often require the collection manager to supervise the process of reducing the footprint of the collection. This can involve weeding, adding compact shelving, moving items to storage, and moving collections online. Modern collection managers, therefore, need to understand the options open to them as well as consummate project management skills, as these projects can involve multiple constituents and a significant amount of oversight.

Leveraging Existing Resources

Happily, the newly appointed collection manager does not have to reinvent the wheel. Standards and formulas already exist that make it easier to measure, house, and assess the collection, and there are established best practices for preserving and maintaining collections. There may be in-house collection development and management policies that can inform storage and deaccessioning activities as well. Information clearinghouses and professional organizations provide time-tested guidance as well as innovative solutions to emerging management issues, and these standards and best practices are referenced throughout this monograph.

Chapter ONE

What You Absolutely Need to Know

For many librarians, the phrase collection management brings to mind the physical efforts of routine stack maintenance: shelving, shelf reading, cleaning, and related activities. In truth, this is a small part of managing a library collection. Stacks maintenance may fall within the scope of a collection manager's position or supervisory role but may also fall to others in the organization. In many libraries, these activities are done by paraprofessionals or student workers. The first sections of this chapter address some of the routine tasks of physical collection management: shelving, maintaining, and securing the collection. The chapter then pivots towards tasks that require data collection, assessment, and evaluation: collection measurement, weeding and storage projects, and other assessment projects. Collection management issues specific to electronic collections are touched upon but covered more extensively in chapter 3.

ROUTINE MAINTENANCE OF PHYSICAL COLLECTIONS

If a collection management library worker is hired to manage an already existing collection, familiarity with shelving options and nomenclature is not immediately necessary. However, it is possible that collection managers will be called upon to rearrange, consolidate, or establish new shelving areas to accommodate changing collections. In those situations, it is important to keep some basic shelving definitions, rules, and recommendations in mind.

Definitions and Notes

A vertical section of shelves is generally referred to as a bay, and a series of bays lined up side by side is called a range or a row. A range can be single faced, which is the case with shelves against a wall, or double faced, when there are shelves on both sides.

Organizing Collections: Discrete collections are housed together, flowing in call number order from the top of a bay to the bottom and from the left side of the range to the right. In public and school libraries, Dewey Decimal Classification is often employed and fiction may be shelved separately by author name, while in American academic libraries materials are most frequently organized by Library of Congress call number. Collections such as government documents may use a separate, specialized organizational scheme and be housed separately.[5] Some libraries may arrange certain materials alphabetically by title. Collection managers should ensure that they are familiar with the organizational schemes used by the institution.

Special Considerations: When ranges are placed non-contiguously, it is important to provide adequate directional signage and make a concerted effort to create a logical flow in the collection. It can help to walk the collection from start to finish and note if there are any areas where it is difficult to identify the next range of shelves in the sequence. If a collection manager is already familiar with the placement of items in the collection, someone with less experience, such as a newer library staff member, student worker, or volunteer, can be recruited to walk the shelves and note any problem areas.

Adequate call number signage on the end caps of shelves provides direction once a library user has navigated to the appropriate area of the library. This signage may be limited to the call number or can contain information on the subject coverage for that range of shelves.

Preparing for New Shelving

In cases of renovation or new construction, a collection manager may be asked to select new shelving for books and other materials. Major library vendors have dozens of shelving designs to choose from. Before selecting shelving for purchase, a collection manager should contact the procurement office (or the equivalent) to find out if there are particular vendors the library works with. The National Information Standards Organization (NISO) publishes standards for library shelving,[6] and given the heavy loads and high use library shelving will receive, it is important to purchase shelving that has met these standards.

Selecting Shelving

If maintaining sightlines or natural light penetration is important, short shelving may be preferred, though it reduces the amount of space available for the collection. Front-facing display shelves can be used to highlight collections or to draw attention to new acquisitions. The two primary styles of shelving include bookcases (i.e., the "traditional" bookshelf made of wood, laminate, metal, or some combination thereof, with an enclosed top and sides) and cantilevered styles, which are generally metal frames with adjustable metal shelves that hang from the frame.

Compact or high-density shelving might be considered in areas where space is at a premium and in closed stacks where library staff will be the primary people accessing the collection. There is a significant cost associated with the installation of compact shelving. There are also structural considerations as the building must be able to bear the increased weight of fully loaded compact shelving.[7]

Limited access collections such as archives, reserves, and special collections can often be stored on higher-density shelving, assuming that delicate and valuable materials are housed in appropriately-sized enclosures. Because of the possibility of injury, moveable shelving is a poor choice for high-traffic collections and children's areas.

LIBRARY SHELVERS AND SHELF READING

Once library collections are adequately shelved, they must be maintained in call number order. It is worthwhile to provide new employees and volunteers with training on both retrieval and replacement of library materials on the shelf. A quick internet search will reveal dozens of online guides to proper shelving by call number, and many libraries create training and orientation materials to explain the classification systems in use.[8]

Training Library Shelvers

One way to check the organizational skills of shelving staff is to present them with a cart of unorganized materials and ask them to arrange the cart in call number order. Patricia Tunstall recommends using training slips: the shelver places a colored slip in each of the books as he/she organizes the cart so that the slips stick out from the top.[9] The supervisor then reviews the cart and discusses any errors that surface. The slips remain in place as the books are reshelved in the stacks. The supervising library worker can follow up afterwards to see whether the items have been placed in the correct location in the stacks. Checking the work of new shelvers the first couple of times they are given the task can help prevent large scale mis-shelving problems. For a more in-depth look at issues related to training and working with library shelvers, Tunstall's *Hiring, Training, and Supervising Library Shelvers* provides a great overview of the hiring and training process, as well as nuanced advice regarding the finer points of supervising, such as creating an environment that values open communication and problem solving.[10]

Shelf Reading

If library staff do not engage in routine shelf reading, which ensures that titles are organized by call number and shelved in the correct collection, a collection manager may want to consider creating this workflow. This can be important in collections that receive heavy use such as children's books, popular reading, and media collections. It is not uncommon for items to be improperly re-shelved, which makes locating items a difficult and frustrating task. Shelf reading will restore order to disorganized shelves and make it easier for patrons to locate materials. Shelf reading can be done in short blocks of time and can serve a dual purpose of identifying and removing items that appear damaged for repair, replacement, or withdrawal. Shelvers can also keep an eye out for preservation issues like mold and pest problems or items that cannot fit on the standard shelving.

When multiple staff members are involved in shelf reading, it is useful to give each person a separate section of the collection to review, or at the minimum, to create a system for indicating which titles have been reviewed in a particular area. Some libraries will place flags, colored slips, or other signage indicating the start and endpoint of reviewed titles, while others may record this information electronically so that the next shelf reader can pick up where the last shelf reader left off. Shelf reading is a continual process and having guidelines regarding both how often an area is reviewed and how long it should take will make it easier for employees to complete this routine task with minimal intervention.

INVENTORYING THE COLLECTION

Taking an inventory requires physically examining the books and comparing them against the library's records using a shelf/inventory list. It is also possible to scan the bar code of items on the shelf and then match those to the catalog records in an item inventory report. The process will uncover previously missing and mis-shelved items; reveal materials in need of replacement or repair; and help ensure that the catalog represents the collection as accurately as possible. Sometimes an inventory will also reveal items that are not in the catalog. This can happen when a misplaced item is assumed permanently lost and withdrawn from the library's holdings.

Often an inventory project is conducted during a low-circulation/ low-activity period because there are fewer items in transit. For school and college libraries, this will usually mean taking inventory over the summer or other vacation period. It may not be feasible or desirable to inventory the full collection at one time; priority should be given to areas with high rates of circulation or missing items. High value or high demand collections, such as art books or local history collections, might also receive priority. Taking a full inventory of each item can be a time-consuming, expensive, and somewhat tedious process. Therefore, many libraries do not undertake routine inventory, but instead analyze a sample of the collection to provide an indication of what percentage of the collection might be missing.[11]

CLEANING AND MAINTAINING THE STACKS

Even organized stacks can be unappealing if they are not routinely cleaned and straightened. Cleaning the collection goes beyond making sure that the areas are free of garbage (generally handled by custodial staff) and aisles are clear. Cleaning of general collections entails vacuuming and/or dusting the volumes and shelves; keeping an eye out for damage from water, mold, and pests; and ensuring that the volumes are shelved properly. Items requiring a deeper cleaning (such as removal of food, gum, or other contaminants) can be removed from the shelf and routed to the appropriate department for cleaning. Depending on the institution, dusting and vacuuming the collections may be the responsibility of the library staff or custodial staff.

Some libraries schedule routine cleaning of specific areas of the collection, while others clean on an as-needed basis. Any materials that cannot withstand routine dusting should be housed in protective enclosures. Fragile and special collections should be treated with care and may require special cleaning materials and handling. Staff members in charge of cleaning these materials should have proper training and follow proper archival guidelines. High-use areas such as children's collections may require more frequent inspection for spills and dirt. In addition, construction projects in or near the library can result in increased dust levels that may require more frequent cleaning in the stacks.

SECURING THE COLLECTION

Most libraries endure a certain amount of loss due to theft or mutilation of library items. There are, however, some basic actions that can be taken to reduce the likelihood of stolen materials. Many, if not most, libraries secure materials using a security system involving magnetic strips or RFID tags attached to materials. These will set off security sensors if not properly processed upon checkout. Security systems are expensive. They require a continual financial outlay for maintenance contracts and the purchase of magnetic strips or tags affixed to library materials. However, despite the not-insignificant initial cost, many libraries find that the reduction in theft makes these systems wise investments.

RFID

While magnetic strips are purely a security measure, RFID tags can replace both the magnetic security strip and the item bar code to provide security and tracking in one device. RFID systems can be instrumental in speeding the checkout process for patrons and in checking inventory. Richard Boss's brief overview of this technology for ALA Tech Notes outlines the advantages of such a system.[12] However, converting from magnetic strips to RFID requires a significant investment of both time and money, and is beyond the budget of many libraries. In addition, because RFID incorporates tracking, it presents patron privacy concerns, though some librarians have worked hard to overcome these issues.[13]

Securing the Physical Space

Even with security gates and item-level security tagging, it may be easy to steal items from the library collection. If the library has windows that can be opened, stealing a book may be as easy as dropping it from a window to be retrieved outside. This risk is mitigated by the installation of screens or security grating that allow airflow without providing an opening large enough to pass a book. Library staff should be trained on how to respond to a security gate alarm and what to do if they suspect a patron of theft. It may be helpful to confer with police or security staff to determine the appropriate response in these cases. Whenever possible, collection managers should ensure that each entrance has a security gate installed and provide active monitoring of those areas.

Securing Media

Media items such as DVDs, CDs, and video games can be placed in purpose-built security boxes that will prevent library patrons from removing the material from the case without assistance. These protective cases are removed upon checkout so that the item is accessible. For easily damaged items such as CDs and DVDs this may also reduce the likelihood that the media will be scratched if someone opens the case while browsing the collection.

Additional Theft Prevention Measures

Even the best security measures cannot prevent all forms of theft. Vandalism can be an issue with expensive and rare items, image heavy materials, and controversial items. Patrons may decide to remove an offending chapter or take an image from a book. In some cases, volumes are vandalized to remove the images or prints to sell to collectors. In academic libraries, textbooks are frequent targets of theft and vandalism. If the library collection contains large numbers of these materials in the open stacks, it may be necessary to create additional security measures, up to and including placing the items on reserve or in a special collection with more careful monitoring. Peggy Johnson in *Fundamentals of Collection Development and Management,* also recommends providing easy access to scanners and photocopiers so that patrons can make copies of the book sections that interest them.[14]

Securing Electronic Resources

Preventing unauthorized access and preserving the integrity of hosted data are two of the most important security issues the library must deal with in relation to electronic resources. In general, collection managers will want to work with IT or systems staff to protect and backup electronic collections and protect patron privacy.

DAMAGE PREVENTION AND COLLECTION PRESERVATION

While damaged materials are an inevitable consequence of well-used library collections, attentive collection management can prevent damage that stems from improper storage, handling, and climate control. At the very least, a collection management library worker should be aware of common preservation issues and familiar with proper storage guidelines. This includes both how materials should be stored on the shelves as well as optimal settings for climate control. If the library has an archivist or a staff member in charge of in-house repair, they can often provide wise counsel regarding proper care of library materials.

Ideal Climate Conditions

The ideal temperature and humidity for the stacks will be determined by material type and by whether the materials are housed in open stacks where people will be present, or whether they will be housed in storage or a closed stack system with limited human presence. In open stacks it is necessary to strike a balance between preservation concerns and human comfort; however, in storage facilities both temperature and humidity may be decreased to improve preservation. As a general rule, temperatures of 65 to 70 degrees are acceptable in general collections and relative humidity should be set between 30 to 50 percent.[15] The humidity should fluctuate no more that 2 to 3 percent from its target, and significant swings in temperature should be minimized.[16]

Climate Control: Discrete areas of the collection require separate climate controls. When there are too few heating and cooling zones in a space it is more likely that some areas will not be kept within desired parameters. Areas that are prone to high humidity may require the installation of dehumidifiers. It is a good practice to monitor temperature and humidity in different zones throughout the day and year to ensure that problem areas are identified. Areas of the stacks that may be fine during the cooler months may become too hot and humid during the warmer months of the year. Large windows without window treatments may make an area uncomfortably hot in bright sunlight or become drafty and let in moisture or pollen and dust from outside.

Adjusting the Library Climate: When the library climate is not within recommended guidelines, it is important to take quick action to prevent damage to the collection. It is much easier (and less expensive) to turn on a dehumidifier for a few hot and muggy days than it is to pay for mold remediation, just as it is less expensive to install a window treatment rather than replace dozens of items that have suffered UV damage. Rapidly fluctuating temperatures will speed up the rate of deterioration of library materials, which can result in warped volumes, damage to images and bindings, and other issues.[17]

Shelving to Reduce Wear: Placement of items on the shelves matters when trying to prevent damage. Shelves should be sized for the materials they are housing. Items should never overhang or rub against the top of the shelf. In addition, books and other items should be stored so that they sit upright on the shelves, but not so tightly that removing an item is difficult. This causes unnecessary wear and can warp bindings. Large books can be stored flat or spine down to reduce the likelihood of the text block separating from the spine, but should never be placed spine up, which results in the text block hanging from the binding, increasing the likelihood of damage. Staff members should be trained to shelve properly and to recognize when shifting is needed.

Insect and Pest Damage: Insect and pest damage is a serious threat to library collections. Often it may be those who shelve and shelf-read who identify potential problems. The first sign may not be a damaged book, but could be droppings, dead insects, presence of an unusual odor, evidence of insect or rodent nests, or other debris in the stacks. Pest infestations can cause extensive damage in a very short amount of time; it is worth familiarizing all library staff with the signs and symptoms. Prevention of infestation can include removal of items that might attract pests such as garbage, food, and clutter; routine dusting and cleaning of the stacks; and ensuring that the exterior of buildings are maintained so that landscaping does not crowd the exterior of the library, creating a potential pest habitat.[18]

The library should have documentation regarding who to notify in the case of an infestation. In some cases this might mean notifying a physical plant manager or maintenance staff; in other situations the library may need to contact pest remediation services directly. This information can be a standalone document or could be part of the library's disaster planning.

DISASTER RESPONSE

Not all collection damage is avoidable. Flood, fire, and other manmade and natural disasters can affect the library's collections regardless of how carefully staff have stored and secured items. For this reason, among many others, the library should have a clearly articulated disaster response plan, outlining the steps to take if the library is subject to a natural or manmade disaster. Obviously, there is a difference between a small water leak or heating malfunction, and a catastrophic event such as an earthquake or fire. The disaster plan should provide enough detail so that staff members can identify the correct course of action given any situation.

Elements of a Disaster Plan

In addition to providing emergency contact and staff evacuation information, the plan should include insurance information and contact information for organizations that can help with disaster mitigation. The Association for Library Collections and Technical Services (ALCTS) maintains an online list of organizations that can help with disaster response and disaster preparedness training (www.ala.org/alcts/resources/preserv/disasterclear). The plan should also outline where any disaster remediation or protective equipment is stored and outline the roles that library staff members are expected to take in the event of an emergency. The plan should identify those in charge of evacuation, retrieval of protective equipment or cleaning supplies, and procedures to follow in contacting organizations or personnel outside the library who will be involved in the remediation effort.

Protecting Personnel: Fire- and flood-damaged items and environments can be hazardous to human health, so proper protective gear should be worn when entering damaged areas, even when they have been determined to be structurally sound. Ensuring that library staff and users are safe and accounted for takes priority over collections-related activities. Any attempts at the salvage of items should only be made after the proper authorities have determined that the area is safe to re-enter.

Salvage Plan: Larger libraries and libraries that house rare or special collections in particular should outline priorities for salvage within their disaster plan. This type of plan provides focus for staff or consultants who enter the library to carry out salvage work. Identifying staff members responsible for coordinating the salvage effort will help provide clarity in a potentially confusing and stressful situation. Outlining a list of materials necessary for the salvage process will also speed up recovery efforts.

Review and Backup: Disaster plans should be reviewed annually to make sure that they are up to date and that the resources and contacts listed in the documents remain valid. Finalized documents should be made available in both print and electronic copy. Ensure that at least one backup copy is available outside the library in case the building or computer servers are compromised.

MEASURING THE COLLECTION

During renovations, space reclamation projects, and other projects that directly impact the amount and location of library shelving, taking accurate measurements of the collection is essential. Failing to correctly capture the size of the collection could mean that there is not enough space to house all materials. This can create additional costs related to moving items to storage, and headaches for staff who may need to shift or weed items more heavily or often than originally planned. Even in the absence of immediate space pressure, administration may wish to understand how much time the library has until the stacks become full. This will involve looking both at the rate of acquisition of materials and measuring the physical collection in relation to available shelving.

Approaches to Collection Measurement

There are several ways to measure collections. Exact approaches involve measuring items on every shelf and accounting for those items that are circulating by using the best estimate of width possible. There are published tables of average width of items in particular subject areas, although there is some question as to whether those tables are transferable from library to library.[19] Less exact methods involve making generalizations based upon a sample or average. Estimates may take less time to calculate but will be less precise. Estimates can be acceptable with small collections, or when shelving is abundant. Librarians can multiply the number of volumes in a particular subject by the average width to come up with a broad estimate of physical collection length. Another estimate involves taking sample measurements to create an average fill rate on each type of shelf, then multiplying that average by the number of shelves to get an estimate of the size of the collection.

Elizabeth Babich's *Moving Library Collections: A Management Handbook* provides an in-depth overview of the pros and cons of exact versus estimated measures, as well as suggested formulas for both types of measurement.[20] There are also readily available articles outlining sampling and measurement procedures to help ensure that the collection measurements are reasonably accurate. For example, Jim Self provides explicit instructions for using sampling to estimate collection size and growth. His method is also adaptable for other collection assessment projects.[21]

Measurement Guidelines

When accurate measurements are critical, it will be necessary to measure every shelf following these general guidelines. First, measure the interior length of each type of shelf in inches. Library shelves are often just shy of thirty-six inches in interior dimensions, but precision matters. Staff should count the number of shelves and then multiply the interior length by the number of shelves.

Each different type or brand of shelving will require a separate measurement. Even when shelves are made of similar materials and look the same at a glance, they may have differing dimensions. Add the various measurements together to get the total shelf space (in inches) available in the collection. Dividing this number by twelve will provide the shelf space in linear feet. In the formula below, it is assumed that there are two different types of shelves. This formula calculates the total linear feet of available shelving, which is necessary in order to determine how much of the available space is currently occupied by the collection. After completing this work, measurement of the actual collection can begin.

FORMULA FOR MEASURING SHELF CAPACITY

(Shelf Type A length in inches × number of Shelf Type A) +
(Shelf Type B length in inches × number of Shelf Type B) / 12 =
Total linear feet of shelving

EXAMPLE

The collection has four shelves with a length of 25.5 inches and six shelves with a length of 39 inches:

(35.5 × 4) + (39 × 6)/12 = 31.33

The total capacity for this library collection is 31.33 linear feet. The next step is to identify how much of this space is taken up by the collection, and how much is free space. One way to determine free space is to measure the amount of empty space on each shelf, adding these numbers together to get total of free space available. Subtracting free space from total shelving space will then provide the space taken up by the collection. Alternatively, one could measure the linear space taken up by materials on each shelf, then subtract that number from the shelving total to give the amount of free space. Once you have calculated either free space or space taken up by materials, it is possible to use the formulas below to calculate total full and empty space on the shelves, as well as determine the percentage of shelving that is filled.

FORMULAS

If X = Total linear feet of shelving, and
Y = Total free space in linear feet, and
Z = Total space taken up by materials in linear feet, then:

The formula for determining total space taken up by materials in linear feet:

X - Y = Z

The formula for determining percentage of shelving that is full:

Z ÷ X × 100

EXAMPLE

If there is 546 linear feet of materials, and 665 linear feet of shelving, then:

546 ÷ 665 × 100 = 82.1 (rounded to the nearest tenth)

Approximately 82.1 percent of the shelving space is full. In this situation, a collection manager would want to consider ways to reduce the space pressure in this collection.

Calculating Growth Rate

Calculating collection growth involves estimating the number of volumes that are added on an annual basis (the acquisition rate), and then calculating the amount of shelf space that these new materials will take up. In *Moving The library: Getting the Collection from Here to There,* Steven Carl Fortriede sets up a methodical and commonsense approach to measuring the size of the current collection and anticipating growth that involves identifying individual collections and making separate calculations for each.[22] While his workflows are predicated on the assumption that one would use this information to design new shelving space for moving the collection, the principles hold for assessing future shelving needs regardless of location.

There is more than one way to look at collection growth. For example:

- Acquisition rate, or the number of items added to the collection over a specific time frame. This may be expressed either as a volume count (e.g., the collection grows by eight thousand volumes per year) or as a percent increase from the previous year's baseline (e.g., the health science collection grew by 5 percent over the previous year).

- Linear feet added to the collection per specific time frame (e.g., the collection grows by 150 linear feet every year).

Acquisition Rate

To calculate the acquisition rate, one identifies the total number of items added to the collection in the time period being analyzed (usually a calendar or fiscal year). It may be useful to take an average over three to five years in order to show general trends. This acquisition information is part of routine reporting in most technical services departments and is often available as a canned report in the library's ILS. Books in some subject areas tend to take up more space than others, and libraries collect more avidly in certain subject areas, meaning that the growth rate and the amount of space needed to accommodate that growth will not be uniform throughout the collection. With smaller collections, this may not be a big issue, but distributing collections appropriately on the shelves in larger collections will be a challenge if differing growth rates are not taken into account.

Calculating physical collection growth requires identifying the average width of an item in the collection. As mentioned earlier, there are published tables that list average width of library materials, but it may be more accurate to calculate averages using the library's existing collection. Finding the average width for an entire collection would be a simple formula (note that the collection is measured in linear feet, while the average width is measured in inches):

If X = Length of collection in linear feet
Y = Number of items
Z = Average width of item in inches

FORMULA FOR DETERMINING AVERAGE ITEM WIDTH
$(X \div Y) \times 12 = Z$

EXAMPLE
If a collection takes up 65 linear feet and is comprised of 520 volumes:
$(65 \div 520) \times 12 = 1.5$

The average width of materials in this collection is 1.5 inches.

It can be helpful to break up larger collections into the smaller component collections, particularly when there is a large difference in volume size between subject areas. One could do this by measuring the call number ranges for different subjects separately. Another approach would be to divide the analysis according to shelf ranges, making note of the starting and ending call numbers. One can then divide the total length of each component collection by the number of items contained in it to determine an average width for that portion of the collection.[23] Accurate measurements depend on making sure items are properly shelved and that items currently in circulation are accounted for. Institutions with cyclical shifts in circulation volume should be measured during the lowest circulation period.

Once a collection manager has both the average acquisition rate (expressed in volumes as opposed to percentage increase) and the average width of the collection being assessed, determining baseline physical growth rate is a simple multiplication of the two numbers.

FORMULA FOR DETERMINING PHYSICAL GROWTH RATE IN LINEAR FEET

If X = Average number of items added per year in a particular range or subject area
Y = Average width of those items in inches
Z =Average growth in linear feet

Then the formula for estimating annual growth is:

$X \times Y/12 = Z$

So if a collection adds 300 items annually and items average 1.5 inches in width, then:

$300 \times 1.5/12 = 37.5$

The collection grows by 37.5 feet per year.

Adjustments to Physical Growth Calculation

In libraries that undergo significant weeding, a collection manager should also make adjustments for how many items are likely to be removed over that same time period, which will slow the overall growth rate. Assessing smaller ranges individually can provide a better understanding of which subject areas tend to grow faster than others. Once a collection manager has determined the baseline growth rate, they may also want to consider additional factors, such as how format shifts and budget adjustments will change the growth rate in the future. Ricky Espinosa provides a sample formula that considers these and additional factors, emphasizing the reality that growth estimates can and will change as internal and external factors fluctuate.[24] When a collection manager has identified a growth rate that seems reasonable for the collection, it can be used to determine how to shift the collection, and how much empty space to leave on the shelves for future growth.

Determining Time to Full Capacity

In some cases determining collection growth is not needed for shifting or space reclamation, but to determine how long it will take for the shelves to reach full capacity. In other words, when will shelf space run out? The best way to get an accurate reading of this is to measure the available space on the shelves for a particular collection, estimate the average annual physical growth rate in that collection, and then calculate the number of years it will take to fill up available space.

FORMULA FOR DETERMINING YEARS TO FULL CAPACITY

Current available space ÷ physical growth rate per year, in linear feet = number of years to full shelf capacity

EXAMPLE

If there is five thousand feet of available space and the library collection grows by two hundred and fifty linear feet per year:

5000 ÷ 250 = 20

It will take twenty years until all available shelves are filled (without embarking on major collection management projects).

Anticipating collection growth is essential to maintaining attractive, usable collections. Knowing the library's shelf capacity, and assessing how close the library is to reaching full capacity, provides information that allows collection managers to identify areas of the collection that need to be shifted or weeded and prevents damage to materials due to overcrowding.

SHIFTING THE COLLECTION

A quick walk-through will provide a general idea of whether the collection is cramped and approaching capacity. Collection areas that are growing quickly should be provided with more empty shelving so that shifting is not a constant process. However, leave the shelves too empty and it will look as though the collection is sparse or that staff have removed materials too aggressively. While there is no hard and fast rule, many libraries aim for around 65 to 75 percent of each shelf to be filled. This allows space for removing and reshelving items as well as for collection growth. Once shelves reach the 85 to 90 percent full mark, it becomes more difficult to shelve and add items to the collection.

Some questions to ask while walking through the stacks:

- How full are the shelves?
- Are shelves left empty?
- Are there particular areas where the collection seems cramped? Are there areas that seem relatively sparse?
- Are there areas where books have been stored in unusual ways due to item size or the congestion of the shelves?

Answers to these questions will help determine whether there is an urgent need to shift collections, weed collections, or make a case for additional shelving and/or storage. Shifting the collection can help redistribute materials and relieve space pressure in areas of the collection that are growing more quickly than others. On the other hand, a walk-through may reveal that there is ample space and more intensive measuring or assessment is not needed. Much like a carpenter will "measure twice, cut once," library staff should "measure twice, shift once" whenever possible.

ASSESSMENT

Using Data to Make Decisions About Your Collections

The work of collection management goes beyond the routine maintenance needs of physical collections and assessments that ensure that the stacks are not overcrowded. Once the collections are in the stacks, the collection manager gathers information to make informed decisions, identify areas in need of attention, and develop an accurate picture of the scope of holdings. A strong collection assessment program can also inform collection development efforts.

Types of Assessment

Assessment of the collection can take many forms. Quantitative assessment options are based on quantifiable or mathematical data. These data provide insights about trends in usage and acquisitions. Common quantitative assessment data include circulation statistics, average age of materials, acquisition rate, weeding and deaccessioning statistics, statistics on items that are damaged and repaired, as well as e-resource usage statistics such as COUNTER reports and session reports.

Qualitative assessments are based on open-ended or unstructured data such as interviews, focus groups, and surveys. These aim to understand how library stakeholders use the collection and what suggestions they may have for improving the usefulness of the library's collection. This type of assessment can uncover areas for further exploration and is good for revealing gaps in the collection or areas where the collection is not meeting user expectation.

Assessment may also be user-focused or collection-focused. User-focused assessments measure usage, usability, and satisfaction with the collection, while collections-based assessments may compare the collection against peer institutions or standard bibliographies, or may assess whether the collections meet appropriate professional or accrediting standards.[25] Many collection managers use a combination of assessment types depending on what questions are being asked and what resources are available.

Creating an Assessment Plan

With the trend towards more assessment and data-driven decision-making in many libraries, there can be a temptation to gather as many kinds of data as possible. However, it is important to make sure that the data one gathers serves a current or foreseeable future purpose. Developing a plan for what you want to measure and how the data will be used can make the collection and reporting of data more meaningful. It may be useful to start with a question or questions you want to answer using the data. For example, are there certain collections that are more vulnerable to theft? Should the library provide both print and electronic copies of the same text?

There are several ways to identify what data to collect. The collection manager should conduct a "data audit" to determine what data is collected and if there are annual reports or surveys to complete. Staff can make an inventory of the regular reports and reviews requested by administration and other entities. If the department is required to produce an annual report, the collection manager should identify the metrics to report. Libraries often participate in annual surveys that require collection data from organizations such as IPEDS, Petersons, and professional organizations to accreditors, consortia, state library boards, and others. In some cases one needs counts or averages, but in other instances comparisons that are more complicated are required. Saving and comparing these reports over time will allow a collection manager to see trends that might not be obvious at first glance.

Using Assessment Data

Data analysis and assessment allow the collection manager to make a variety of decisions about the collection. For example, a quick analysis of the publication dates in the computer sciences might reveal that titles are generally over ten years old. For most popular circulating collections these would be considered outdated and of little use. The titles could be moved to storage or weeded. The collection manager might then notify collection development staff to make sure there are adequate current materials in the collection. Using assessment data to identify areas in need of collection development is beyond the scope of this book. However, open-ended, qualitative assessment such as focus groups or interviews will reveal collection gaps or subject areas that are out-of-date or in poor condition. When a subject area is out-of-date or, conversely, exhibits unusually high circulation rates, collection development staff should be notified to ensure there are sufficient quality materials to meet patron demand.

Ultimately, the collection assessment program should be tailored to the unique needs of the organization. If assessing the collection falls within collection management responsibilities, the collection manager should focus on making sure the collection reflects the needs of the user population and supports the library's mission. Because collection evaluation takes both money and time, it is important to have a goal in mind. Is analysis necessary to compare the holdings against similar institutions, determining relative strengths and weaknesses? Is electronic journal assessment required in anticipation of cancelling subscriptions due to budget cuts? Should staff interview young adults to determine their thoughts about the popular reading collection? What questions you are trying to answer will determine which approach to data collection and analysis you take.

WEEDING THE COLLECTION

Of all collection management activities, weeding, or removing items from the collection, seems to engender the most stress, reluctance, apprehension, and even fear. These negative feelings can stem from the fear of accidentally removing the wrong book or a deeply held belief that all library materials have value. Collection managers may be concerned about a possible negative response from library users. Some librarians prefer using less fraught terminology for this process, such as pruning, deselecting, and discarding. Regardless of the terminology used, the space constraints in the library, migration to online formats, and the nature of many subject collections mean that in most libraries, weeding is a critical part of proper collection management.

Properly executed, a weeding program will identify collection items that are outdated, out of scope, damaged, presented in archaic formats, or otherwise unnecessary, such as surplus copies of a once-popular text that is no longer in demand. Librarians review items and then remove them from the collection if they meet pre-identified criteria. Weeding can also uncover mis-shelved items or items that require attention in the form of re-classification, repair, or relocation.

Planning a Weeding Project

An organized weeding process begins with planning. Assessing the scope of the project, creating a timeline, and establishing a plan for communicating with library stakeholders is essential. The collection manager should identify all of the staff members who may be involved in the process, and make sure each one is aware of their particular role. If multiple units of the library are involved, staff should have clarity regarding the workflow and each unit's role in the process. Testing the proposed workflow by walking a title through the process provides an opportunity to see how the steps will work and to identify any steps that may need to be revised for efficiency.

Outlining the procedures for title review and defining parameters for what to keep and what to discard ensures that all members of a weeding project team are on the same page. Additionally, planning for the physical removal of library materials is important, whether the idea is to recycle, donate, or sell discarded items. Government institutions are often limited in how they may dispose of property, so collection managers are wise to explore this issue before beginning a project in earnest.

Weeding Criteria

If not already in place, the library should identify weeding criteria that will help those who are reviewing materials make sound decisions regarding what remains in the collection. Established guidelines also facilitate communication with stakeholders who may have questions about how and why items are identified for weeding.

Common criteria for determining whether to weed an item include:

- Age of the item
- Circulation statistics
- Relevance to the community or to the curriculum
- Rarity and the importance of the published work, including awards and mentions in highly regarded bibliographies
- Number of other institutions that hold the item (to ensure availability via ILL)

- Condition of the item
- Currency of information
- Inclusion of offensive or biased terminology
- Not every library considers all of these factors, and some may have additional criteria not represented here. The important thing is to identify the key metrics for making withdrawal determinations and to ensure staff members are looking at enough of the key metrics to make well-informed decisions.

Most integrated library systems can run reports listing materials that fit broad subject, age, and circulation parameters, and library staff can then further refine the list using the full criteria and their professional expertise. For example, titles of local or regional interest, valuable and classic works, are often retained regardless of current use or age. Some public libraries may have weeding guidelines that place heavy emphasis on recent circulation (or lack thereof), whereas academic libraries that are focused on curriculum or research support may decide on more lenient age or circulation thresholds for materials.

Checklists

One popular school of thought regarding weeding is to compare the list of titles under consideration for withdrawal against a standard checklist of key titles in that area. Checklists might include award winners or standard works in a field. Professional organizations often provide these lists on their websites or in publications for purchase. *Choice* produces the annual "Outstanding Academic Titles" list, and many libraries avoid weeding titles that appear in this list. Librarians managing fiction collections might retain titles that have received a major literary award. However, the particular needs and mission of the institution could and should supersede a static list of recommended titles. In other words, if the title is no longer relevant to the library's programs or constituents, it may be a candidate for removal regardless of reviews or accolades.

Collection Analysis Services

Collection analysis services such as OCLC's WorldShare Collection Evaluation (www.oclc.org/en/collection-evaluation.html) and Sustainable Collection Service's GreenGlass (www.oclc.org/en/sustainable-collections.html) are software tools that are useful in comparing the library's print collection against similar institutions, which can be helpful for weeding and storage decisions as well as for collection development. These services can also be helpful when participating in a shared print project.

In a shared print project, the library works cooperatively with other libraries, usually in the same region, to ensure that access to materials is maintained. Each participating library agrees to maintain specific titles and is responsible for replacing these titles if they are damaged, lost, or stolen. This way, low-use materials can be weeded by most participating libraries with the assurance that the title is still available from the institution that has pledged to maintain holdings. Since the burden of maintaining holdings is spread among all participating libraries, there is less pressure on individual libraries to maintain comprehensive, "just in case" collections. If a collection manager works in a library that participates in a shared print project, it is essential to know which titles must be maintained.

Physical Review

While physical review of titles is time-consuming, it can be a great way to understand the weeding process and get to know the collection. Physical evaluation of titles can also reveal the condition of materials. Some librarians pull titles and review items on a cart, while others review items in the stacks, pulling or marking only the items that require further attention. Ways of marking titles include placing distinctive stickers on the spine, tipping the titles on their sides, and inserting paper flags. Many libraries use slips to indicate the disposition of reviewed titles. Options may include:

- Weed the item
- Update the item with a newer edition or similar title

- Send to repair
- Send to storage
- Send to technical services for relocation/call number adjustment/etc.

This information can be printed or written on a physical slip to place in each book or the decision can be noted on a spreadsheet for later action. Determining which approach is best depends on the scope of the weeding project, the materials and equipment available to reviewers, and whether there is adequate storage for loaded book carts. It is also useful to include the following information for each title (regardless of whether library staff are using digital or analog systems):

- Title/author
- Call number, barcode, or other identifying number, such as OCLC number
- Reason for weeding
- Specific repair work that is required
- Name of reviewer

Secondary Review

In academic libraries it is good practice to allow faculty some measure of review over the materials identified for removal. Librarians may choose to communicate directly with departments or place lists of titles under review on websites or library guides and then solicit feedback. If the library has a liaison program, working with designated subject liaisons can provide reassurance to faculty that the library is not making weeding decisions without consultation. Some libraries establish department-level collection policies with faculty, which can then serve as a guide for weeding the collection. Making weeding documentation publicly accessible also makes it easier to respond to any questions or complaints library staff may receive about the weeding process.

Public libraries may use "last chance" displays of titles under withdrawal consideration. In these displays, if a title circulates, it stays, and if it does not, it is removed. This can provide some transparency in the weeding process while also allowing patrons to feel as if they have some say in what stays in the collection.

Removing Weeded Materials

When removing items from the collection it is important to be sensitive to how the process can look to library users and members of the public. Boxing items for removal may be more labor intensive but potentially less disruptive than tossing books in large bins or dumpsters. It only takes one alarmed patron to spread the word that the library is "trashing" its collection. However, some librarians favor a more open approach, saving and displaying particularly egregious examples of outdated materials in order to help communicate the necessity of weeding or submitting them to online galleries such as Awful Library Books (https://awfullibrarybooks.net/why-weed/).

SELECTING ITEMS FOR STORAGE

Libraries have limited physical capacity, and in many cases, the collections eventually exceed the space available. Rather than weeding items to fit within the space, many libraries choose to move lesser-used items to storage, particularly in research institutions where the long-term retention of items for future scholarly use is part of the mission of the institution. This storage may be in high-density shelving somewhere onsite or may be located in an offsite storage facility or library annex.

The process used to identify titles that are likely candidates for storage can be quite similar to the process used to identify candidates for weeding. The emphasis when moving titles to storage is to identify titles least likely to circulate. Collection managers may also consider storing duplicate copies and materials that are available online or widely available from other nearby libraries. Collection managers should be aware of the time it will take to retrieve items from storage; this could have an impact on the parameters set for whether to place an item in storage. For rare or delicate materials it may make more sense to move the item to a special collection rather than place it in storage with the regular circulating collection. Storage facilities should have proper climate control and adequate staffing to make sure the collection is properly shelved and maintained.

CHANGING COLLECTION FORMATS

The shift from a predominantly print-based collection to expanding electronic collections is well underway in most libraries. Collection managers may be asked to assist in reducing print collections, maintaining remaining print collections, and managing problems with access to electronic collections. To effectively manage changing formats it is important to understand the implications of switching from physical formats to online and to understand some of the terminology used for electronic resources.

License Agreements

In general, the license agreement for an electronic resource outlines who can access the content, where and how they can access the content, and what restrictions exist for sharing or re-use of content. Licenses might also address perpetual access rights, or lack thereof. It is important to note that licenses can be negotiated, and in some cases must be negotiated, particularly if the library is a state institution that requires specific licensing language. The Liblicense project (http://liblicense.crl.edu/) provides advice, guidance, and model license templates for those who must negotiate licenses with library vendors. In some cases, license negotiation is handled or supervised by acquisitions, the purchasing department, or legal counsel affiliated with the institution. License agreements should be maintained in a file either electronically or in print for easy access and referral. The Interlibrary Loan Unit in a library may also need access to or copies of license agreements.

Temporary Versus Perpetual Access

Licensed content is only accessible from the library for the duration of the license agreement, unless there is a clause within the agreement that identifies perpetual access rights. This is common with many online journal subscriptions: a license might provide access to the past ten years of a journal, but only provide perpetual access to the content that was published during the year(s) the library subscribed. Depending on the specific details of the license, even if the library has purchased perpetual access to content, the publisher may charge an annual hosting fee.

For research collections, ensuring perpetual access can be of significant concern. Organizations such as JSTOR and Project Muse have created durable agreements with publishers to serve as archives of content. So if the library subscribes to these collections, a collection manager can be confident that the content will not disappear. The organization Portico also provides reliable access to electronic content when publishers cease operating, no longer host back issues of a journal, or discontinue titles. While a small portion of Portico's collection is open access, there is a fee to become a full participant in the program. The Portico website (www.portico.org) provides a full listing of participating publishers and instructions on how to participate. LOCKSS (Lots of Copies Keep Stuff Safe), based at Stanford University, is another digital preservation program that creates a network of locally held content that can be provided when the publisher hosted content is unavailable. Like Portico, publishers must sign an agreement allowing LOCKSS to preserve content and make it available to participating libraries.

Aggregators Versus Publishers

In general, publishers provide original content such as books, magazines, and journals, while aggregators (EBSCOhost, ProQuest, Gale) provide access to content from multiple publishers. Sometimes publishers will withhold the most recent edition of a book or issues of a journal from aggregator platforms for a specific period of time (the embargo period). This funnels purchase requests directly to the publisher during the period when the content is in highest demand, which increases revenue for the publisher.

Aggregators provide publisher content in a variety of ways. As mentioned above, some aggregators, such as JSTOR, provide permanent archival access, while others provide content based on regularly renegotiated licensing agreements. EBSCOhost and ProQuest products generally follow this model. An aggregated database provider that does not promise archival access might lose the rights to host content when publisher agreements shift. If the library has made storage or discard decisions based on this access, the institution runs the risk of losing content when licensing agreements are changed or cancelled. However, because the electronic resource landscape is in constant flux, access is rarely permanently lost. Archives may be available for purchase or subscription on another platform, or through organizations such as Portico and LOCKSS.

MANAGING ELECTRONIC COLLECTIONS

Managing electronic collections involves a whole host of issues that are not present when dealing with physical collections. For many libraries, management of electronic resources falls to a separate unit within the library. Physical collections are straightforward to manage in that items are usually purchased, processed, shelved, circulated to one user at a time, and repaired as needed until they are removed from the collection. Even book leasing programs, such as the popular McNaughton program, are straightforward in that items are leased and returned based on patron use and collection size. Borrowing and use policies for physical collections are set by the library following institutional guidelines.

Electronic items, on the other hand, may be purchased, leased, or made available for potential use within the catalog, hosted by the content provider or downloaded for hosting on a local server, available on the open web, bundled together in packages and aggregated databases, or available a la carte on a title-by-title basis. Each publisher/aggregator sets parameters for what constitutes appropriate use and who counts as an authorized user. Management of electronic collections is therefore largely focused on staying on top of content changes, ensuring records are discoverable, managing changes to access, ensuring links work, and assessing usage and cost trends to make data-informed decisions about subscriptions.

E-Resource Management Overview

Once an electronic resource is acquired, designated library staff work to activate the resource. This can include configuring authentication via proxy or other method, providing IP and other network information to the vendor, adding records to the catalog or selecting the content in a knowledgebase so that content is visible, and providing links to content in a database directory or research guide. Each step in activating an electronic resource may involve systems, technical services, acquisitions, and collection development librarians who may each oversee a portion of the process. All of these processes have implications for collection managers who must ensure that links work and records are updated when subscriptions change or materials are weeded.

Maintaining Access in a Changing Landscape

Publishers and aggregators continue to explore new ways of displaying and organizing content for users. In the process, some collection management issues are solved and some new concerns are introduced. For many libraries, perpetual, reliable access to online content in a format that retains the original layout and images is the gold standard. For text-based resources such as journals this has typically meant PDF format that duplicates what an item may have looked like in print. However, there are accessibility concerns for PDF content since image-only PDF documents are not compatible with screen-reading software. Document accessibility is a growing concern among US universities and colleges, and some have instituted policies that prevent the purchase of materials that are not made available in an accessible format. Accessibility of documents is a question that should be discussed with the vendor before signing the license.

CHAPTER **TWO**

Standards, Guidelines, and Best Practices

New collection managers may be reassured to learn that there are widely accepted standards and guidelines published by professional organizations for just about everything one might encounter. Many standards are outlined by specific divisions within the American Library Association, while others are generated by state government, library consortia, or other professional organizations.

Awareness of library standards can help to ensure that libraries maintain the level of service required by accreditation or certification bodies and, in a more practical sense, can save time and energy when performing common library tasks. There is no need to reinvent the wheel. In fact, one might consider it a "best practice" to perform a search for related standards and guidelines whenever embarking on a new collections-related project. Unless the project is on the cutting edge for collection management, chances are other librarians have dealt with a similar project.

BASIC CONSIDERATIONS

Collection managers should become familiar with the general collections-related standards of their library type (K–12 school, academic, public, or special). In addition, collection managers will need to be familiar with standards relating to:

- accessibility of physical and online collections
- standards relating to the reporting of usage metrics and report format for collection assessment
- standards relating to housing and maintenance of library materials

Defining Standards and Guidelines

The American Library Association (ALA) has moved away from prescriptive standards for libraries, recognizing that different types of institutions require different approaches towards collections, services, and programs. Instead, the Association's divisions and units provide standards that are relevant to the area of librarianship the division represents. The ALA Standards webpage (www.ala.org/tools/guidelines/standardsguidelines) identifies divisions that may publish relevant standards for the library or collection type. ALA does make a distinction in the definitions of standards and guidelines. The current online Standards Manual provides clear definitions, quoted below:

> The ALA Policy Manual (55) defines standards as, "policies which describe shared values and principles of performance for a library." Standards documents:
>
> a. Tend to be comprehensive, covering a broad scope of programs and services provided by a library.
> b. May define both qualitative and quantitative criteria.
> c. Present goals toward which the profession aspires.
> d. May include statements expressed in relative terms; that is, by relating library performance to norms derived from a reference population.
> e. Set criteria for the decisions and actions of those concerned with the planning and administering and accrediting of library services.

The ALA Policy Manual (55) states that guidelines "consist of procedures that will prove useful in meeting the standards." Guideline documents:

> a. Are program- or service-specific and not necessarily comprehensive.
> b. Define qualitative criteria; generally exclude quantitative criteria.
> c. Identify factors contributing to program effectiveness.
> d. Provide a framework for developing service policies and procedures.
> e. Incorporate benchmarks by which a particular library and information service, resource, or material may be judged. (www.ala.org/tools/guidelines/standardsmanual/manual)

In general, standards originate from organizations and government entities, rather than individual libraries or institutions. Standards outline the requirements that institutions must meet to ensure a minimum level of service. While all standards are not applicable to all libraries, it is important to know which standards apply to the specific institution type. In addition, sometimes standards that are not necessarily required of the institution can serve as useful indicators for best practice. Even if the library is not *required* to adhere to certain preservation standards, for example, it might still be a good idea to reference them when trying to figure out how to preserve the collection.

Quantitative Versus Qualitative Standards

Quantitative standards set minimum requirements for collections and may be determined by metrics such as the ratio of items to population served and baseline numbers of periodical subscriptions, physical volumes, or database subscriptions. Maintaining relevant quantitative standards in the face of shifting formats, the increasing role of free internet resources, and changing research habits has become an ongoing challenge. There has been a shift away from these sorts of prescriptive standards, particularly at the top level of organizations.[26] Instead, many library organizations are moving towards qualitative assessment; rather than asking whether a collection has the required minimum number of items, these standards ask whether the collection adequately serves the needs of the target population. Assessing the success of a library's collections can be more challenging using qualitative methods, but this allows for more flexibility in adjusting the collection to shifting needs, priorities, and formats.

Guidelines

Guidelines provide advice on how institutions might go about meeting standards. Guidelines are generally not required but can serve as a useful starting point for establishing proper collection management procedures. Guidelines may be tailored to fit the needs of the individual institution.

STANDARDS FOR PUBLIC LIBRARIES

Standards for public libraries are generated by state governments. The state library, board of library commissioners, or library consortia may publish standards for a particular state.[27] They can encompass minimum standards for collection size, service hours, or programs, and may be qualitative or quantitative in nature. For example, in the Commonwealth of Massachusetts, public libraries are subject to minimum standards requiring that the institution participate in interlibrary loan and reciprocal lending.[28] Public libraries must meet this minimum standard, or risk being de-certified, which will prevent libraries from receiving state appropriations. However, the specific way in which the libraries go about achieving this goal is left open. In Massachusetts, a network of nine geographically distinct resource-sharing consortia issue guidelines for resource sharing for member libraries, and it is through membership and participation in these consortia that most public libraries in Massachusetts are able to meet the state standard.[29]

STANDARDS FOR ACADEMIC LIBRARIES

ACRL Standards

The Association for College and Research Libraries (ACRL) publishes the *Standards for Libraries in Higher Education*, which outlines principles and performance indicators for academic libraries. The most recent revision of the *Standards*, approved in 2018, does not make significant changes to collection standards from previous versions.[30] Collection managers should pay particular attention to the principle related to collections, quoted here.

> Performance indicators for academic library collections include the following (numbering from the original document is included):
>
> 5. Collections: Libraries provide access to collections sufficient in quality, depth, diversity, format, and currency to support the research and teaching missions of the institution.
>
> 5.1 The library provides access to collections aligned with areas of research, curricular foci, or institutional strengths.
>
> 5.2 The library provides collections that incorporate resources in a variety of formats, accessible virtually and physically.
>
> 5.3 The library builds and ensures access to unique materials, including digital collections.
>
> 5.4 The library has the infrastructure to collect, organize, provide access to, disseminate, and preserve collections needed by users.
>
> 5.5 The library educates users on issues related to economic and sustainable models of scholarly communication.
>
> 5.6 The library ensures long-term access to the scholarly and cultural record.[31]

The standards document also contains an appendix (Appendix 1) with sample outcomes to assist libraries in developing a method to assess how well the institution is adhering to the principles. Explanatory text outlines how to write effective outcome statements. The standards are intentionally written so that libraries can create flexible assessments, taking into consideration the particular institutional priorities and curricular and research needs of the user population. Finally, Appendix 2 of the *Standards* is devoted to benchmarking and peer comparison, providing sample metrics that might serve as useful markers for comparison.

ACRL also publishes guidelines relating to the transfer of items from academic general collections to special collections which are available at www.ala.org/acrl/standards/selctransfer.

ACCREDITATION STANDARDS

Institutions of higher education can be accredited at the institutional level, as part of a regional accreditation, as well as at the program level. Both regional and programmatic accrediting may involve qualitative and quantitative library collections standards. A collection manager should be aware of which regional body accredits the institution as well as which academic programs are accredited separately. While library standards for programmatic accreditation can be quite vague, allowing for wide latitude in assessment, they may also be quite specific, indicating required resources or specific benchmarks that must be met for successful accreditation. Accreditation is renewed at regular intervals, requiring institutional self-study and the submission of an accrediting report. If the institution is in the process of renewing its accreditation, it can be immensely helpful to read previous library self-studies to understand what types of assessments were used in the past.

STANDARDS FOR SCHOOL LIBRARIES

The American Association for School Libraries (AASL), the ALA division focused on school libraries, does not generate standards or guidelines for collection management.[32] Instead, school librarians and school media specialists should look to their state governments, state library or board of library commissioners, the Department or Board of Education, or other relevant state organizations for standards and guidelines. Other groups such as the National Association of Independent Schools may accredit school libraries at private institutions. Collection managers interested in general school library standards may consult AASL's *National School Library Standards for Learners, School Librarians, and School Libraries*, most recently updated in 2018.

COMMON CORE STANDARDS

The Common Core State Standards are a set of learning standards focused on English Language Arts, literacy in History/Social Studies, Science and Technical Subjects, and Mathematics. These standards do not specifically address school library collections, but those collections do support school curricula centered on the Common Core. The website for the Common Core provides the full text of the standards, which may be important for collection assessment, weeding, and other collection management initiatives (www.corestandards.org/).

STANDARDS FOR SPECIAL LIBRARIES

Due to the wide variety of institutions that fall under the special library umbrella, there are not the same type of broad standards for special libraries that there are for academic, public, or school libraries.[33] Instead, special library collection managers may need to identify relevant standards and metrics for assessment through research or by identifying the professional organization affiliated with their specific subset of special library. For example, the Medical Library Association publishes the *Standards for Hospital Libraries*, which outlines both quantitative and qualitative standards for library resources, termed "knowledge-based information" or KBI (www.mlanet.org/page/standards). These standards, because they are specific to hospital libraries, are much more relevant and useful than generic special library standards would be. It is beyond the scope of this book to list all possible types of special library standards, but the resource section at the end of this monograph lists a few places to begin research.

STANDARDS FOR ACCESSIBILITY

American with Disabilities Act (ADA) Standards

Library spaces must adhere to the standards outlined in the American with Disabilities Act, most recently updated in 2010. In some cases, older libraries may have spaces that do not comply with the current guidelines but fall under the "Safe Harbor" provision in the 2010 ADA revision. The Safe Harbor provision allows noncompliant structures built before March 15, 2012, that are compliant with the 1991 version of the Act, to remain without alterations. However, if the structure is renovated or new construction is approved, it must be brought into compliance with the current guidelines.[34] The full text of the ADA Standards is available online. It includes numerous illustrations that help to clarify the text, and enumerates the exceptions that come into play in certain facilities.[35] While older versions of the ADA Guidelines incorporated a separate section specific to libraries, under the newest edition these recommendations are folded into the general guidelines outlined in chapter 4.

Aisle Width

Of particular relevance to collection management is section 403, which defines the minimum width of accessible walking surfaces, including stack aisles, as 36 inches.[36] Previous versions of the accessibility standards indicated that a width of 42 inches was preferred for library stack aisles. However, the new standards indicate that 42 inches of clearance is only necessary when the accessible route requires a 180 degree-turn around an object that is less than 48 inches wide. This can often be the case in the stacks area of a library when maneuvering around shelving units.[37] Even in this case there is an exception: if the turning area provided is 60 inches wide or more, then an aisle width of 36 inches is considered adequate.[38] For new construction, planning for 42-inch-wide stacks would be ideal, as a wheelchair could then maneuver around ranges with relative ease. There is no prescriptive minimum or maximum height for library shelving.

The 2010 standards also include information on door width and clearance that may be of importance in the stacks areas of the library. The standards for door width are best accessed on the site directly, as numerous illustrations and examples are presented to explain what is considered ADA compliant.[39]

WEB ACCESSIBILITY STANDARDS

In the United States, there are two organizations that publish standards and guidelines that many librarians look to when assessing accessibility of electronic resources: 1) Section 508 Standards for Electronic and Information Technology of the Rehabilitation Act of 1973 (Section 508) and 2) the Web Content Accessibility Guidelines (WCAG).

Section 508: The Section 508 standards are federal standards outlining requirements for technology accessibility for people with disabilities. While the standards technically only apply to resources procured by the federal government, in practice they have become broadly accepted as appropriate standards in both the private and public sector. In addition, several states and institutes of public education have adopted the standards. This means that some libraries may be required to ensure electronic resources meet the standards, while other institutions may have some leeway in providing resources that are not compliant. The Section 508 Standards were "refreshed" in early 2017, with a compliance date for federal agencies of January 18, 2018.[40]

WCAG: WCAG, developed by the World Wide Web Consortium (W3C), are voluntarily adopted by web developers, but have achieved broad international consensus. The most recent version is WCAG 2.1, which was finalized in June 2018 (www.w3.org/WAI/standards-guidelines/wcag/). The Section 508 refresh was made with older WCAG 2.0 in mind, as those were the guidelines in place at the time of the re-fresh.[41] For collection management purposes, both sets of accessibility standards can serve as one facet of evaluation when reviewing electronic collections, be they aggregated databases, multimedia collections, eBooks, or journal subscriptions. In particular, collection managers should note whether databases and other online content are accessible to those using assistive technology such as screen readers.

When electronic resources and technologies are labeled as Section 508 or WCAG 2.1 compliant, it is an indicator that the resources meet minimum standards for accessibility.

CHAPTER **THREE**

Things You Might Encounter

This chapter outlines things you may encounter relating to creating and maintaining collection policies, and physical and electronic collection management issues beyond those addressed in the second chapter of this book.

COLLECTIONS-RELATED POLICIES, PROCEDURES, AND REPORTS

From both a practical and theoretical standpoint, clearly written policy and procedural documents save a collection manager time and provide needed clarity when questions arise. Collection policies outline the philosophies, rules, and guidelines that the library adheres to relating to collections, while procedures provide directions on how to accomplish tasks.

Locating and Reviewing Existing Documentation

Documentation can save a collection manager time when approaching a new project; streamline the staff training process; and ensure that all library staff members are approaching collection management tasks and projects in the same way. Many libraries have binders or online documentation outlining common library procedures in an easy to understand, step-by-step process. In particular, it is extremely helpful to locate the following:

General Library Policies, Plans and Statements

- The library's mission, vision, and values statements (if they exist). The library's mission and values should inform the collection manager's activities, while the vision will provide background on the library's intended future direction.
- The library's current strategic plan, if available, is an important document that provides information about the mission and vision of the institution as well as evidence of institutional priorities and goals.
- Collection development policies at the general and subject or genre-specific level. While this volume does not cover collection development, these policies may include valuable information that may impact collection management activities such as deselection criteria.
- Preservation, storage, weeding, transfer, and/or deselection policies.
- Any policies relating to collection accessibility.

Common Collection Management-Related Procedures

- Tracing procedures for locating lost/missing items.
- Routine shelving procedures, including shelf reading, re-shelving, and any inventory procedures.
- Weeding procedures and/or workflows.
- Collection management workflows (these are helpful particularly when more than one person is involved in managing the lifecycle and access of a library resource).

- Claiming procedures (particularly important if the collection manager is responsible for serials).

Review and update policies and procedures to ensure they remain in line with current practices. At the policy level, updating or changing the written document will likely require review and approval by the library director, and may involve others depending on the type and structure of the library.

Creating New Policies

If it is necessary to write policy from scratch, remember that policy documents should be clear, concise, and focused. They will serve to guide library staff and can also help library users and other stakeholders understand the role of the library. Policies should be written for a broad audience, avoid professional jargon, and clearly explain library-specific ideas or terminology. Reviewing other institution's policies is a useful exercise, both to understand the scope of what is covered and to identify policy elements that should be included or eliminated from the library's own policies. Electronic discussion lists and online forums can also be great resources for finding sample policy documents, as many librarians are happy to share what has worked for their libraries.

Collection Management Reports

Collection managers may be asked to write reports for both internal and external audiences. In general, if the audience for a report is external it is important to avoid library jargon and to write clearly and concisely. If the report contains significant amounts of quantitative information, a collection manager may consider using data visualizations such as charts and graphs that will help convey important points. For longer reports, a one- or two-page executive summary can highlight the main findings and key statistics. This will ensure that the most important elements of the report are conveyed even if the recipient does not have the time to carefully review the full report.

COLLECTION MANAGEMENT CONCERNS FOR PHYSICAL COLLECTIONS

Proper Housing and Storage

Each range should have adequate bookends or book supports (many shelves have an adjustable wire support that hangs from the top shelf) so that materials sit squarely and are not leaning one way or another on the shelf. Leaning can place tension on the spine and warp the binding. Book spines should be flush with each other and line up along the front edge of the shelf.

Some collections, such as children's materials and games, maps, and ephemera can be challenging to store on standard library shelving. Special storage cases for maps and other large, flat items are necessary to prevent damage to the collection while maximizing accessibility. Games may require the purchase or construction of protective cases or storage bins to ensure pieces stay together. Rigid or semi-rigid file cases can protect loose magazines, journals, and other easily bendable media from distorting on the shelf.

If oversized materials are scattered throughout the collection, a collection manager may consider collocating them in a designated oversize collection to maximize shelving efficiency. Large or oversized books that cannot fit on the shelf spine-out should be stored flat or in large-format/oversize shelving. These items may also be shelved spine down to decrease wear on the spine.

Media items can also be challenging to store on standard shelving, particularly if security cases create an irregular shape. These may require special shelving accessories to help prevent them from tipping over or slipping behind other items in the stacks. For this reason, interfiling media items such as CDs or DVDs with monographs can be problematic. Some libraries shelve media separate from the main collection to ensure efficient use of shelving space or so that specialized media shelving can be used to house the materials.

Damaged Items

Many larger libraries have their own in-house preservation and repair staff, and smaller libraries may have staff members trained in preservation and repair techniques. Other libraries rely on outside vendors who will repair and/or rebind materials. Rare and archival materials should be assessed and repaired by a preservation professional, and the specialized skills and standards for this type of repair are beyond the scope of this book. Basic repair steps are easy to teach to paraprofessionals, student workers, and volunteers and can be a relatively low-cost way of extending the life of library materials.

If the library does not have a designated conservation or preservation department, knowing how to properly repair a torn page or tighten a hinge can help extend the life of the circulating collection. The Northeast Document Conservation Center (NEDCC) holds regular classes and webinars on basic preservation skills for paper and media items. While the multi-week online course is available for a fee, the center makes the textbook available at no cost, allowing even those without significant professional development funds to learn about basic care and handling of materials (www.nedcc.org/free-resources/preservation-101). There is also an excellent, clearly written manual about basic book repair available from the Ohio Preservation Council and the State Library of Ohio.[42]

If written descriptions of repair techniques are not sufficient, many basic repairs are clearly demonstrated through YouTube videos. Library supply companies such as Demco, Brodart, and Gaylord provide basic book repair kits that include essential repair items such as transparent page repair tape, cloth binding tape, hinge repair tape, acid-free glue, and tweezers. When significant repair work is anticipated, purchasing a book press can be a good investment, though using flat, straight boards and bricks or other weights can serve the same purpose.

Tracing Lost and Missing Items

Library materials reported as missing from the shelves should be recorded as such, and an attempt should be made to locate or "trace" them. Items that cannot be located upon the first pass are held and searched again after an appropriate time has passed. The frequency and number of tracing attempts is largely up to the individual collection manager to decide. Eventually, if the item is not located, it is permanently removed from the collection.

A library tracing procedure document should:

- outline which staff members are notified when an item goes missing;
- describe what is done to locate the item, including the frequency of search and the interval between attempts to locate the item; and
- detail how long the record is kept in the catalog before the item is replaced or removed.

There are no hard and fast rules here. One library might replace items immediately if an initial search does not turn up the item, or if it has been requested by a patron, while another library might put the item in a trace queue and fulfill the immediate request through interlibrary loan. Some libraries choose to suppress lost item records, while others prefer to keep them visible with a status of "lost" or "missing." It is a good practice to forward the list of missing items to the collection development staff for review and possible replacement.

MANAGEMENT CONCERNS FOR ONLINE COLLECTIONS

Online collection management presents special challenges. The variety of formats, purchase and leasing models, and rapidity in product development in this area means that best practices are still emerging and evolving particularly when it comes to issues such as deaccessioning and accessibility. Adding confusion to the process, demand-driven and pay-per-use access models for many electronic resources can make it difficult to define electronic collections and determine what constitutes ownership.

eBooks

A long-term management concern for eBooks is how to handle weeding perpetual access titles when they no longer fit with collection guidelines. Often library staff can work with the publisher or vendor to suppress the content if it is available through a platform or database, and then the record can be suppressed or withdrawn from the ILS. Suppressing a record may not always prevent the item from appearing on the vendor platform, but it will make the content less discoverable. For library-hosted items, removing content is simpler as it will involve library staff removing the record, the link, and deleting any digital content residing on servers.

License Models

Leased eBooks are often limited to one user at a time, although some providers have an unlimited, simultaneous user purchase option. In cases where unlimited access is not available, libraries may have to pay more for increased access. This may mean upgrading to a two-, three-, or five- user license for a title, purchasing additional single user "copies" of an eBook, or purchasing another higher tier of access as determined by the publisher's purchase model. Most vendors can provide usage and turnaway reports that can be used to make collection management decisions.

Digital Rights Management (DRM)

Digital rights management is an extra layer of protection against eBook piracy that limits what can be done with the material. Generally, DRM titles can be downloaded for a limited period of time and cannot be copied or shared easily, though portions may be made available for download or printing. DRM can complicate the process of accessing eBooks and severely limit the ways in which the content can be used and shared. Some publishers provide DRM-free materials, which are preferable due to their ease of use and flexibility in viewing and sharing content on multiple devices.

Evidence Based, Demand Driven, and Patron Driven Acquisition

Increasingly aggregators and publishers are providing new, data-driven models of acquisition. In patron-driven (PDA) and demand-driven (DDA) models, libraries make content available via links in the catalog or knowledgebase, but do not purchase the content until a trigger event (usually a certain number of uses of a particular title). In some models, the library commits to purchasing a certain dollar amount of material after a period of time and then looks at usage to determine which titles to purchase. The library then loses access to titles that were not purchased under the agreement. In some cases, a PDA or DDA trigger event will automatically generate a purchase and in some cases it will place the title in a shopping cart or list for library review, deactivating content for users until a purchase decision has been made.

Evidence based models exist for eBook, eJournal, and streaming media content, and each model varies in terms of what qualifies as a "use," how many uses might trigger a purchase event, and whether the purchase is mediated or unmediated. Evidence-based acquisition can provide access to a much larger collection than could be purchased outright. From a collection management perspective, the challenge is ensuring that the library maintains access to purchased content even as unpurchased content access changes. Communicating how these models work to library users can also be a challenge and may require the creation of explanatory guides or FAQ.

Electronic Journals

The management of individual electronic journal subscriptions and electronic journal packages involves many of the same issues that come into play with eBooks. Electronic journal content can be obtained through annual subscription, one-time purchase, or demand-driven article level purchase. Managing eJournal collections involves staying abreast of any content or licensing changes during renewals, as well as monitoring usage to confirm that library resources are being spent efficiently. Maintaining accurate URLs is also crucial, since website upgrades, publisher mergers, and title transfers from one publisher to another can all affect journal content access. Collection managers may be able to automate some eJournal maintenance by using an online knowledgebase such as WorldShare Management's Collection Manager or ProQuest's 360 Core.

Managing eJournal Budgets

One of the biggest issues surrounding management of electronic journals is how to manage annual cost increases that average 5 to 8 percent, particularly when library budgets remain relatively stagnant.[43] Many libraries are now in the position of scaling back monograph purchasing and cutting low-use or exceptionally expensive subscriptions to stay within budget. In the absence of a dedicated electronic resource department, collection managers may want to be proactive by assessing journal usage and having a plan for determining which titles could be cancelled should the need arise. Some librarians have found that moving to a pay-per-article model (either mediated or unmediated) cuts down on costs significantly,[44] but it also cuts down on owned content. In most models of pay-per-particle, online access is not perpetual but limited to twenty-four to forty-eight hours. Frequently, pay-per-article (and ILL fulfillment) results in direct delivery to the library patron, which minimizes the role of the collection manager. However, a collection manager may still be called upon to explain the system to patrons or troubleshoot access, particularly if a PDA/DDA plan is in place. Open-access journals have grown tremendously in the last decade, and collection managers may want to discuss how these journals are selected for addition to the collection as well as how access points are managed.

Aggregated Databases

Aggregated databases, such as those licensed by EBSCO, ProQuest, and Gale, also have collection management implications. Two of the most frequent management concerns with these resources have to do with changing URLs and changing publisher agreements, which can mean dramatic changes in the content of these resources. From a management standpoint, it is important to stay on top of these updates so that seamless access to content is maintained and changes are communicated to constituents. In some cases, loss of key content from an aggregated database might trigger a review of the subscription or an exploration of alternative ways of licensing that content.

Some database providers, particularly archival collections such as JSTOR and Project Muse, require that publishers maintain access to the content provided, which means there is typically less volatility in the content of these databases.

Streaming Media

Much like eBooks, streaming media can be licensed via aggregated collections, licensed individually for a specific period of time or licensed with a one-time fee for perpetual access, often with an annual hosting fee. Aggregated streaming media providers must continually negotiate access and licensing with various distribution companies. This means the available content on these platforms is in a constant state of flux, similar to content in aggregated journal databases.

Assisting Patrons with Using Electronic Media

In environments where multi-media content may be embedded in other webpages, such as research guides or course management software, it may be necessary to provide guidance on how to properly embed or link out to the content. Accessibility of these collections is also a concern. Video collections should provide closed captioning or transcripts of the audio content, and all collections should be compatible with screen reading software.

OTHER ONLINE COLLECTIONS—REPOSITORIES AND BEYOND

Libraries increasingly own or provide access to additional online collections that pose management issues. Institutional repositories, archives, data sets, and open educational resources (OER) are some of the many online collections that libraries may administer and manage. Some of these collections are hosted on library or institutional servers and their maintenance and management can involve technical services staff, IT, subject specialists, archivists, scholarly communications specialists, faculty members, and others. New collection managers should clarify whether their responsibilities extend to management of any of these types of collections. The particular challenges specific to managing institutional repositories, archives, and the like are beyond the scope of this monograph, though the chapter on resources includes some useful links.

Free Online Content

Ideally, a collection development policy outlines how free online resources such as government and nonprofit databases are selected and made searchable by the library, whether they are added to an online knowledgebase, cataloged, or included in a directory of library resources such as an A-Z database list. Free online content should be periodically assessed for access (broken links, problematic design, and accessibility) and continued relevance to the collection. Some of this work can be automated, but often requires examining the site. Maintaining significant numbers of free resource links and records requires staff time and energy, and maintenance can fall by the wayside when the management of physical and subscription-based resources takes priority. It pays to be selective and think through how the library approaches this type of collection.

The library may also link out to other institutions' repositories, archives, and other online collections. A collection manager may have some responsibility for determining how and when these collections are represented in the library's holdings. As with other free web resources, keeping up with changes to links and assessing the currency of these collections is necessary.

Usage Statistics

Collection managers are often responsible for collecting and analyzing usage data for electronic collections, so it is important that they understand the types of usage data they might encounter. Many companies report usage using metrics and formats differently; one of the challenges when assessing electronic resources is ensuring that similar metrics are compared across products. To help create uniformity in usage data reporting, Project COUNTER (Counting Online Usage of NeTworked Electronic Resources) has created standards for counting usage in electronic resources. The project defines what counts as "use" under various parameters and standardizes the format of how this data is presented. As of January 2019, the most current version of COUNTER, Code of Practice Release 5 (COP5), provides reports at the Platform, Database, Title, and Item level (www.projectcounter.org). The standard reports a vendor provides will depend on the particular resource being analyzed. COP5 departs significantly from previous standards in order to simplify the reporting process and to provide flexibility so that COUNTER can adapt to the changing electronic resources landscape. The Project COUNTER website provides extensive documentation on past, current, and future implementations of the Code of Practice.

Accessing Usage Reports

Most library vendor's COUNTER reports can be downloaded manually, scheduled for delivery, or automatically harvested using the Schemas for the Standardized Usage Statistics Harvesting Initiative (SUSHI) protocol. The reports can then be manipulated or uploaded into an analytics platform. Despite attempts at standardization, even COUNTER-compliant usage reports can include inconsistencies in formatting and content that can make analysis difficult. Cleaning up the data files is often a necessary part of gathering usage statistics.

There are some companies that do not employ standardized usage reports. In these cases, it may be possible to identify metrics that are broadly similar to categories that are defined in COUNTER. In other cases, the lack of standardization will make true comparison of usage nearly impossible. These resources will need to be evaluated based on publisher-provided metrics or by reaching out to users to find out the perceived value of the resource.

CHAPTER **FOUR**

Tools of the Trade

Given the scope of a collection manager's potential duties, there are a myriad of skillsets and tools one might need to accomplish both routine and specialized tasks. Here is a brief selection.

THE BASICS

The Microsoft Office suite, particularly Excel and Word, and its analogues, such as Google Docs and Sheets, are key tools for productivity as a Collection Manager. A thorough knowledge of your library's ILS and any reporting features it contains are essential. Collection analysis and evaluation software can also greatly simplify collection management projects.

PROJECT MANAGEMENT

Every collection manager needs to be able to propose, plan for, and execute projects of all sizes. Much of the heavy lifting in this position will come in the form of large scale projects, such as space reclamation projects that require significant downsizing of the print collection, assessment of print and electronic collections to identify gaps or mismatches between current collection development policies and the existing collection, new library additions, shifting, and the opening of offsite storage facilities. If a collection manager has never had the opportunity to manage a project in the library, a few keys documents and tools can help tremendously in making sure new projects are successful.

The Project Outline

At the most basic level, the project outline should include:

a. the goal of the project
b. the key internal and external personnel required to complete the project and the tasks they will be expected to perform
c. a project timeline, including both beginning and ending dates
d. an estimated budget if applicable

The project outline may also include a rationale, cost/benefit analysis, or a statement on the anticipated benefits or efficiencies created by undertaking the project. This is especially important if the project is reviewed and approved by library administrators, in which case it might be better to think of this document as a project proposal rather than an outline. There should be a clear argument articulating why the project should move forward.

Project Management Software

Project management software can streamline planning and provide a record of the project's progress. This is particularly useful as projects become more complex and involve larger numbers of staff. A dedicated project management application can make it very easy to record and visualize discrete project tasks, assign those tasks to particular staff, and ensure that each step of the project is finished. Microsoft Project uses the Gantt chart, which creates a timeline of all tasks and allows the user to mark off what is completed. There is also a wealth of project management apps that integrate with Google Apps, including Wrike, Mavenlink, and Zoho Projects.

Project-Related Documentation

Written guidelines and procedures reduce questions and discrepancies in interpretation of the steps in a project. For example, when weeding the collection, it is helpful to develop documents that outline review criteria, identify required supplies, describe routing procedures, and specify steps for maintaining records and statistics. Separate documents, such as decision trees or checklists, provide structure for the actual review process.

Any staff participating in the project should be able to understand the documentation as written and perform tasks as outlined. Of particular importance is making sure there are no missing steps in workflows. Test the documentation with staff by running through the steps with a sample from start to finish. This provides an opportunity for staff to ask questions and get clarification on any ambiguous instructions.

Progress Reports

The collection manager should communicate regularly with those who are participating in the project and those supervisors or administrators who oversee the library or the unit. In a small institution, small informal check-ins can be useful. In a large library or when overseeing a particularly ambitious project, building in a regular schedule for updates will help prevent budget and timeline related surprises.

Final Project Summary

At the close of the project, write a brief summary that outlines the results. What was the final cost? How long did it take? How many volumes were moved to storage/relocated/inventoried/etc.? This information may be included in an annual report or added to a portfolio of accomplishments for employee evaluations or serve as a record for future projects of a similar nature.

No project plan is infallible. Construction, time, and budget estimates are only guesses at what it will take to complete a project. Collection managers should know what to do if the project will not be finished on time or for the initial projected cost and speak with the appropriate library staff to explore options for completion. In some cases, a hard deadline will require more resources directed to finishing a project. In other cases, overly ambitious planning may mean that a reduction in the scope of the original project or timeline extension is necessary. It is better to address budget and timeline problems as soon as they appear than to wait until the last minute, hoping something will change.

LIBRARY WORKFLOWS

Workflows are important because they bring standardization and clarity to tasks and make apparent who is responsible for what aspects of an activity. Well-written workflows can assure that nothing falls through the cracks. Information regarding who handles each step of the workflow is not absolutely essential, but it can provide great clarity for those involved in the process.

In general, a workflow contains the following information:

The triggering event. An item is purchased, a request is made, or a decision to perform a particular activity is made.

Task and routing information. Once initiated, who is responsible for the various steps? What are the steps? This should be brief but fairly specific and might include tools or software that are needed to accomplish the task, though it should not outline the actual process for accomplishing the task. The process is better described in a procedures document. An example in a bulleted list might read "the collection manager will collect COUNTER reports DB1 and DB2, normalize the data, and upload them into the Usage Analysis platform." This might also be broken up into three discrete steps. A separate procedures document could explain how the collection manager should go about collecting COUNTER reports DB1 and DB2.

Decisions points. Often, at some point in a process a decision is required. The outcome of that decision will determine the next step in the workflow. For example, in a subscription review situation, the decision to continue a subscription entails one set of tasks, while a decision to cancel entails a separate set of tasks. Different staff members and departments might be involved depending on decisions made.

Information on how the workflow ends. This could either be the final task in the workflow or, for cyclical workflows, information on when the cycle is repeated.

A simple workflow can be written out in a list or bullet points. Often, it can be helpful to create flowcharts or other visualizations to see how the task progresses from one step to another. The SmartArt feature of Microsoft Word can be particularly useful for visualizing workflows. There are also many publicly available workflow apps such as Monday.com and SmartQ.

It may seem like a small detail, but it can be helpful to write workflows (as well as other policy and procedure documents) using the title of the staff member rather than his or her name, so that staff turnover doesn't make the workflow confusing or obsolete.

Given the complexity of managing electronic resources, documenting workflows in this area can be of particular use. In some electronic resource management systems, it is possible to set up a workflow so that the relevant staff will be notified when it is time to perform their assigned tasks.

ANALYTICS AND DATA ANALYSIS TOOLS

Collection managers, like many types of librarians, must be able to examine and analyze large amounts of data. While high-level technical skills are not absolutely required for this, the more facility one has with Excel, various analytics platforms, basic statistical analysis and even coding languages, the quicker and more easily one can come to conclusions about the collection. Using an analytics tool can greatly reduce the amount of time spent manually analyzing the data, with the added benefit of producing data visualizations and tracking trends automatically.

If a collection manager only masters one of these applications, Excel or a similar spreadsheet-focused app such as Google Sheets is probably going to be the most useful. Excel makes it easy to share analyses with a wide group of stakeholders through the export of charts and other visualizations into documents, presentations, or for display on websites. Basic analytical formulas include cost-per-use (cost for a particular time period divided by the number of usages during that time period, which might be searches, views, downloads, or some other metric) and use or cost trends over time (particularly helpful for subscription-based resources).

Library-Specific Analytics Tools

EBSCO's Usage Consolidation, Intota Assessment, Springshare's LibInsight and OCLC's GreenGlass provide collection managers with the ability to assess return on investment, identify high- and low-use resources, and make well-informed decisions regarding the disposition of materials. These are only a handful of the many analytics platforms made by library-focused companies.

Other Analytics Tools

Non-library specific tools that are helpful for analyzing large amounts of data and creating visualiza-tions include OpenRefine (https://openrefine.org/), Tableau (https:/www.tableau.com/), and R (https://www.r-project.org/). These somewhat complex programs provide flexibility and a level of customization that simpler out-of-the-box options do not have. There is extensive documentation on how to work with these apps available on the web. Simple data visualization is also possible with Microsoft Excel.

CHAPTER **FIVE**

Relevant Resources

The following section contains resources for further education about collection management tasks and issues, as well as information on opportunities to connect with other librarians responsible for collection management.

Professional Organizations

Association for Library Collections and Technical Services (ALCTS)

While ALA and other professional organizations maintain interest groups and roundtables dedicated to collection management, ALCTS has collections as a primary focus. The Collection Management Section deals specifically with collection management issues, providing online education opportunities as well as interest groups based around particular types of library or collection management activity. (www.ala.org/alcts)

Northeast Document Conservation Center (NEDCC)

NEDCC is a conservation lab as well as a clearinghouse for information related to the preservation and conservation of materials made of paper or parchment. (https://www.nedcc.org)

Society of American Archivists

Provides information and training related to archives and preservation. (www2.archivists.org)

Conferences

Many large professional conferences such as the ALA Annual Conference, the ALA Midwinter Meeting & Exhibits, ACRL Conference, and AASL National Conference offer sessions dedicated to collection management issues. The conferences listed here routinely provide a wide variety of programming relevant to collection managers.

ACRL Assessment Conference

A biennial conference focusing on the assessment of all aspects of library services, including print and electronic resources. (https://libraryassessment.org)

Altmetrics Conference

Not limited to a library worker audience, this conference is for anyone who works with altmetrics- expect a mix of publishers, researchers, and institutional sponsors as well. (www.altmetrics conference.com)

Charleston Library Conference

While subtitled "Issues in Book and Serial Acquisition," this conference presents information on the changing landscape of publishing and is particularly relevant for learning about changes in format and new developments with content providers. (https://charlestonlibraryconference.com)

ER&L—Electronic Resources & Libraries

An annual conference focusing on managing all aspects of electronic collections, including selection, renewal, assessment, and more. (www.electroniclibrarian.org/conference-info)

Online Courses

As with most aspects of librarianship, there is now a wealth of online courses, both free and tuition-driven, that provide information about collection management and provide a forum for discussing collection management issues with other professionals in the field. A small selection of these types of courses, suited to a beginning collection management librarian, are outlined here.

ALCTS Online Learning (courses, webinars, and e-forums)

Courses include Fundamentals of Collection Development and Management, Fundamentals of Preservation, and more. Webinars focus on building coding and other technical skills, providing updates on changes in the field, and special topics in collections and technical services. Webinars older than six months are available to view for free on the ALCTS YouTube channel: www.youtube.com/user/alctsce. (www.ala.org/alcts/confevents)

Library school-based offerings

Many library schools offer special continuing education courses or allow non-matriculating students to take individual courses on a continuing education basis.

Library Juice Online Courses

Library Juice provides low-cost coursework focused on building practical skills. Collection Managers may find courses in the "Reference and Collection Development" or the "Cataloging, Technical Services, and Coding" areas of interest. (https://libraryjuiceacademy.com/index.php)

Electronic Discussion Lists

Most electronic discussion lists can be accessed directly via the web and subscribed to using RSS or e-mail. These lists can be an excellent way to find out about national and regional professional development events as well as a way to connect with other professionals who are focused on collection management topics.

Alcts-eforum

This electronic discussion list hosts monthly two-day forums on topics relevant to collection management, collection development, and technical services. Recent forums include topics such as managing large-scale weeding projects, preservation, and electronic resources management. (https://lists.ala.org/sympa/info/alcts-eforum)

Alcts-eres

This electronic discussion list focuses on all aspects of e-resources acquisition and management. (https://lists.ala.org/sympa/info/alcts-eres)

ALSC Children's Collection Management Discussion Group

Specifically focused children's collections. Presents meeting agendas and information on ALSC events relevant to collection management. (https://connect.ala.org/alsc/home)

Coll-assess

This electronic discussion list focuses on collection assessment and best practices for evaluating collections. (https://lists.ala.org/sympa/info/coll-assess)

Coll-dv

This electronic discussion list focuses on all aspects of collection development and management. (https://lists.ala.org/sympa/info/colldv)

Digi-pres

This electronic discussion list focuses particularly on issues around digital preservation and conversion. (https://lists.ala.org/sympa/info/digipres)

Uniaccess: ACRL Universal Access Electronic discussion list

This list focuses on accessibility issues. Most of the postings focus on web accessibility with some discussion regarding accessible library services and physical collections. (https://lists.ala.org/sympa/info/uniaccess)

A Selection of Journals and Articles Related to Collection Management

Collection Management. Taylor & Francis. Print ISSN: 0146-2679 Online ISSN: 1545-2549

Journal of Electronic Publishing. Ann Arbor, MI: University of Michigan Press. ISSN 1080-2711

Journal of Electronic Resources Librarianship. Taylor & Francis. Print ISSN: 1941-126X Online ISSN: 1941-1278

Library Resources & Technical Services. Chicago: American Library Association. ISSN: 2159-9610

Physical Collection Management

See the Endnotes section for those items specifically referenced within the text.

Digital Commons Network. Collection Development and Management Commons

Provides an access point for browsing or searching a number of institutional repositories with content related to managing library collections. (http://network.bepress.com/social-and-behavioral-sciences/library-and-information-science/collection-development-and-management)

Frase, R. M. & Waxter, S.G. (2013) Taking stock: Shelf space and allocation.

Public Libraries Online. Retrieved from http://publiclibrariesonline.org/2013/04/taking-stock-shelf-space-and-allocation/

Electronic Resource Management

Robin Chin Roemer and Rachel Borchardt. "Keeping Up with Altmetrics." *ACRL website* www.ala.org/acrl/publications/keeping_up_with/altmetrics

Liblicense Project

This project provides a model license as well as a discussion forum for those involved with negotiating licenses for their institutions. (http://liblicense.crl.edu)

Project COUNTER

Project COUNTER publishes standards for usage reporting.

The website includes in-depth information regarding upcoming changes to the standards. (www.projectcounter.org)

TERMS (Techniques for Electronic Resource Management)

The TERMS project "aims to set out the e-resource life cycle and to define a set of best practice using real world examples gathered from libraries in the UK and US." TERMS 2.0 includes preservation for the first time. (https://library.hud.ac.uk/blogs/terms)

Institutional Repositories and Digital Collections

"ACRL Scholarly Communication Toolkit: Repositories."

ACRL LibGuides (https://acrl.libguides.com/scholcomm/tool kit/repositories)

bepress Digital Commons Resource Library.

(www.bepress.com/products/digital-commons/resources/resource-library)

Jane D. Monson, *Getting Started with Digital Collections* (Chicago: ALA Editions, 2017).

Resources for Locating Standards

"ALA standards and guidelines" (www.ala.org/tools/guidelines/standardsguidelines)

"AALL Public Policies," *American Association of Law Libraries*, www.aallnet.org/mm/Leadership-Governance/policies/PublicPolicies.aspx.

"Guidelines and Standards for Technical Services" (www.ala.org/alcts/resources/guides)

"ISO 11799:2015: Information and documentation—Document storage requirements for archive and library materials," *International Organization for Standardization,* www.iso.org/standard/63810.html.

Margaret Bandy et al., "Standards for Hospital Libraries 2007," *Journal of the Medical Library Association* 96, no.2 (2008): 162-169, www.ncbi.nlm.nih.gov/pmc/articles/PMC2268237.

"Public Library Standards by State," *Public Library Statistics Cooperative Wiki,* http://plsc.pbworks.com/Public-library-standards-by-state.

"Collections Care: Preservation Guidelines for Digitizing Library Media" (www.loc.gov/preservation/care/scan.html)

Epilogue

Successful collection management is the result of careful, attentive physical maintenance of the collections, accurate data gathering and assessment, data-informed decision making regarding the disposition of physical and virtual items, continual professional development, and effective project management. As with many jobs in the library, collection management is often a collaborative task, requiring teamwork, delegation, and clear communication. While the collections and physical space of the library continue to evolve, many of the elements of effective collection management remain the same: providing security, ensuring accessibility, identifying items in need of attention, and assessing the usefulness and relevance of collections. The increasing availability of software programs and cloud-based solutions can streamline management processes, but it is up to collection managers to determine how best to leverage new tools and new formats to fill the needs of their user population.

About the Author

BECCA BRODY is the Head of Library Collections and Content at Westfield State University's Ely Library in Westfield, Massachusetts. She received her MSLS from UNC-Chapel Hill's School of Information and Library Science and an MPA with a concentration in Non-Profit Management from Westfield State University.

SERIES EDITOR

SUSAN E. THOMAS currently serves as the ALCTS Monographs Editor. She is also the Director of Collection Services for the Schurz Library and Subject Librarian for the Health Sciences at Indiana University South Bend. Susan has 27 years of experience working in academic libraries. Prior to her current position at IU South Bend, Susan served as the Facilitator for Reference Services and Archivist (1995–1997) at Valdosta State University (Georgia), the Assistant Head of the Regents Center Library and Bibliographer for Social Welfare at the University of Kansas/Edwards Campus, and as a Medical Reference Librarian at the University of Oklahoma Health Sciences Center Library. Susan holds a B.A. in Psychology (Indiana University), a Master's in Library and Information Science (Indiana University), and a Master's in Public Affairs (Indiana University South Bend).

Endnotes

1. For example, see G. Edward Evans and Margaret Z. Sapponaro, *Collection Management Basics,* 6th ed. (Santa Barbara, CA: Libraries Unlimited, 2012), and Peggy Johnson, *Fundamentals of Collection Development and Management*, 3rd ed. (Chicago: ALA Editions, 2014). The utility of Johnson's work on collection development and management cannot be overstated. In addition to both theoretical and practical discussion, the extensive references, resource section and glossary provide an excellent grounding in the scholarship and specialized language of collection management.
2. Evans and Sapponaro, *Collection Management Basics,* 20.
3. Ibid.
4. Johnson makes this distinction in *Fundamentals of Collection Development and Management.* While she covers both processes, she identifies collection management as those activities that happen after materials have been acquired.
5. "Superintendent of Documents (SuDocs) Classification Scheme," Federal Depository Library Program, accessed August 23, 2017, www.fdlp.gov/catalogingand classi fication/cataloging-articles/1791-superintendent-of -documents-sudocs-classification-scheme.
6. NISO, *ANSI/NISO Z39.73-1994 (R2012) Single-Tier Steel Bracket Library Shelving,* approved by NISO, January 2012, accessed June 13, 2017, www .niso.org/apps/group_public/project/details.php?project_id=83.
7. See William W. Sannwald's *Checklist of Library Design Considerations* (Chicago: ALA Editions, 2001) for a list of items to consider when choosing standard, compact, or automatic retrieval shelving.

8. An easy way to locate these items is to perform a Google search with "Library of Congress Classification Tutorial" or "Dewey classification tutorial" for search terms.
9. Patricia Tunstall, *Hiring, Training, and Supervising Library Shelvers.* (Chicago: American Library Association), Chapter 3, accessed July 13, 2017, https://e-bookcentral.proquest.com.
10. Ibid.
11. For a discussion how to select a sample for a variety of collection assessment activities, see: Jim Self, "Using Sampling to Assess Library Collections," (2001), accessed June 30, 2017, www.arl.org/component/content/article/6/1931.
12. Richard W. Boss, "RFID Technology for Libraries," *ALA Tech Notes*, (2004), accessed 7/6/2017, www.ala.org/PrinterTemplate.cfm?Section=technotes&Template=/ContentManagement/HTMLDisplay.cfm&ContentID=68138.
13. David Molnar and David Wagner, "Privacy and Security in Library RFID: Issues, Practices, and Architectures," in *Proceedings of the 11th ACM Conference on Computer and Communications Security* (New York: ACM, 2004), 210-219.
14. Johnson, *Fundamentals of Collection Development,* 232.
15. Northeast Document Conservation Center (NEDCC), "Preservation Leaflet 2.1: The Environment: Temperature, Relative Humidity, Light, and Air Quality: Basic Guidelines for Preservation," accessed July 25, 2017, www.nedcc.org/free-resources/preservation-leaflets/2.-the-environment/2.1-temperature,-relative-humidity,-light,-and-air-quality-basic-guidelines-for-preservation.
16. Johnson, *Fundamentals of Collection Development,* 230.
17. NEDCC, "Preservation Leaflet 2.1."
18. "Pest Control" in *Library Preservation and Conservation Tutorial*, Cornell University Library, accessed May 9, 2017, www.library.cornell.edu/preservation/librarypreservation/mee/management/pestcontrol.html.
19. Elizabeth Chamberlain Babich, *Moving Library Collections: A Management Handbook.* (Westport, CT: Greenwood, 1998), 21-23.
20. Ibid., 3-10.
21. Jim Self, "Using Sampling to Assess Library Collections," (2001), accessed June 30, 2017, www.arl.org/component/content/article/6/1931.
22. Steven C. Fortriede, *Moving Your Library: Getting the Collection from Here to There.* (Chicago: American Library Association, 2010), 34-39.
23. Ibid., 44-48.

24. Ricky Espinosa, "It's All in the Numbers: Calculating the Growth of Collections and Spaces," *American Libraries* (September 2015), accessed June 28, 2017, https://americanlibrariesmagazine.org/2015/09/10/its-all-in-numbers/.

25. Johnson, *Fundamentals of Collection Development,* 302.

26. "Library Standards," American Library Association, accessed July 12, 2017, www.ala.org/tools/atoz/library-standards.

27. See the resource section labeled "Resources for Locating Standards" at the end of this monograph for more information.

28. "Regulations and Standards," Massachusetts Board of Library Commissioners, accessed July 13, 2017, https://mblc.state.ma.us/programs-and-support/state-aid-and-aris/regs-standards.php.

29. "Library Networks," Massachusetts Board of Library Commissioners, accessed July 13, 2017, https://mblc.state.ma.us/programs-and-support/library-networks.php.

30. See the draft copy available at http://connect.ala.org/files/Standards%20for%20Libraries%20in%20Higher%20Education.comments.5noappendices.pdf.

31. The Association of College and Research Libraries, *Standards for Libraries in Higher Education,* approved by the ACRL board of directors, February 2018, accessed May 25, 2018, www.ala.org/acrl/standards/standardslibraries.

32. Evans and Sapponaro, *Collection Management Basics,* 142.

33. Brent Mai, "Measuring for Success," *Information Outlook* 16, no.5 (2012), 3-4, accessed August 10, 2017, www.sla.org/IO/2012/Sept-Oct/IO-SepOct2012.pdf.

34. "Overview of Revised Regulations," ADA National Network, accessed May 25, 2018, https://adata.org/factsheet/overview-new-regs.

35. United States Department of Justice, *2010 ADA Standards for Accessible Design,* accessed August 4, 2017, www.ada.gov/regs2010/2010ADAStandards/2010ADAStandards.pdf.

36. Ibid, 117.

37. Ibid., 118.

38. Ibid., 118.

39. Ibid., 119-127.

40. United States Access Board. "About the ICT Refresh." Accessed August 29, 2017, www.access-board.gov/guidelines-and-standards/communications-and-it/about-the-ict-refresh.

41. Ibid.
42. Ohio Preservation Council, *Basic Book Repair Manual*, (2009), accessed July 10, 2017, http://opc.ohionet.org/opcjoomla/images/stories/bookrepairmanual.pdf.
43. Stephen Bosch and Kittie Henderson, "Fracking the Ecosystem: Periodical Price Survey 2016," *Library Journal* 141 no.7 (2016), accessed August 10, 2017.
44. Douglas K. Bates, "Individual Article Purchase: Catching the Wave of the Future, or Getting Pounded on the Reef," *Proceedings of the Charleston Library Conference* (2013), accessed September 10, 2017, http://docs.lib.purdue.edu/cgi/viewcontent.cgi?article=1455&context=charleston.

CPSIA information can be obtained
at www.ICGtesting.com
Printed in the USA
JSHW061922160523
41671JS00008B/173

9 780838 946640